ZGODBA ŠTEVILK

SMALL BOOK ONE

ENGLISH - SLOVENIAN

---

*Numbers Teach Children
Their Number Names*

written and illustrated by

MISS ANNA

Early Reader Edition of *The Number Story 1*
Bronze Medal Winner, 2016 Wishing Shelf Book Award

Library of Congress Control Number: 2018902040

Names: Miss Anna, author.
Title: Number story : numbers teach children their number names / Miss Anna.
Description: Portland, OR: Lumpy Publishing, 2018.
Identifiers: ISBN 978-1-945977-46-6 | LCCN 2018902040
Summary: The pictures and rhymes present stories which introduce numbers 0-10.
Subjects: LCSH Numeration—English--Slovenian--Pictorial works--Juvenile literature. | BISAC JUVENILE NONFICTION /
Languages: English--Slovenian
Classification: LCC QA141.3 .M57 2018 | DDC 513—dc23

Publisher: Lumpy Publishing
Website: www.missannabooks.com
Email: missanna@missannabooks.com

Paperback: ISBN 978-1-945977-46-6
Printed in the U.S.A.   1 3 5 7 9 10 8 6 4 2

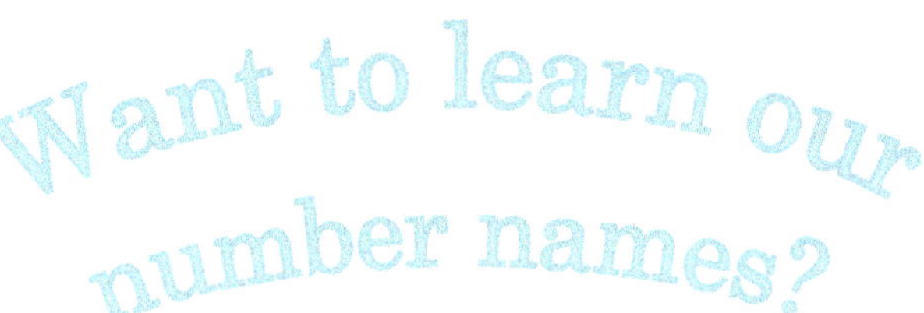

Bi se rad naučil
imena številk?

It is very easy and a lot of fun!

Zelo zabavno je, in čisto nič težko!

Say-along our little jingle

Zapoj z nami našo zgodbico!

starting from Number One!

Začeli bomo s številko ena!

1

ONE   looks like my one finger.

ENA

izgleda kot en moj prst.

ONE!
ENA!

2

TWO   trails a tail.

DVA

ima rada rep.

A TAIL! REP!

3

THREE has bumps.

TRI

ima dve buški.

BUMPY! BUŠKI!

4

FOUR carries a sail.

ŠTIRI

napihuje se kot jadro.

A SAIL!
JADRO!

5

FIVE   is a racing track.

PET

je dirkalna steza.

VROOM
BRUUM!

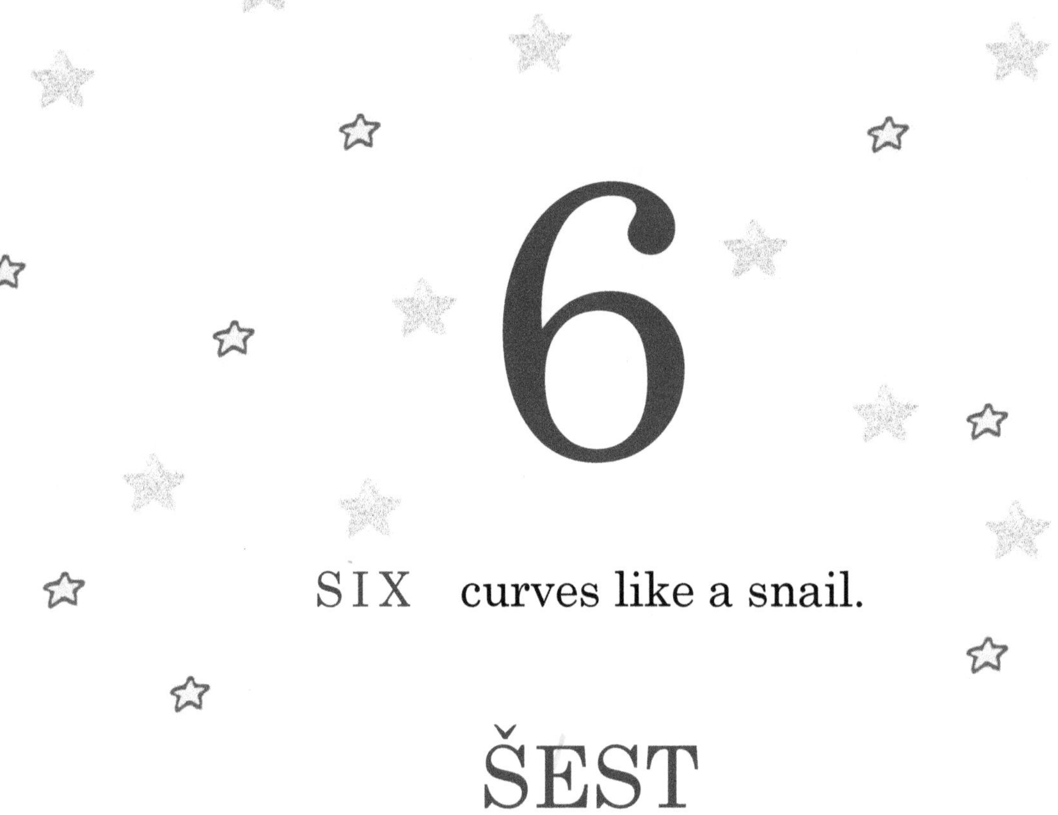

SIX   curves like a snail.

ŠEST

izgleda kot polž.

A SNAIL! POLŽ!

7

SEVEN has a sharp angle.

SEDEM

ima ostri rob.

OUCH!
AUČ!

8

EIGHT   is rollercoaster rails.

OSEM

je kot proga vlakca smrti.

JUUUPIIII!
YIPPEE!

NINE is a bubble on a stick.

DEVET

je mehurček na palici.

A BUBBLE! MEHURČEK!

10

TEN is an eye of a whale.

DESET

je kot kitovo oko.

WINK!

POMEŽIK!

And
In
0
ZERO   is an empty pail.
NIČ
je prazna posodica.

IT'S EMPTY!
PRAZNA JE!

Thank you for playing with us today.

We had a lot of fun too!

Hvala ker ste se danes igrali z nami.

Me smo se zelo zabavale!

We are your Number friends,
Zero to Ten,
Who will be here for you~
Smo tvoje prijateljice številke
od nič do deset.
In vedno bomo tukaj zate.

Bye-bye now!
See you again soon!
Adijo za zdaj!
Kmalu se spet vidimo!

The Numbers are *SINGING* too!

To sing-a-long, look for Miss Anna Number Story
at your favorite music store like iTUNES.

MP3

Numbers 0-10
IDENTIFYING & COUNTING

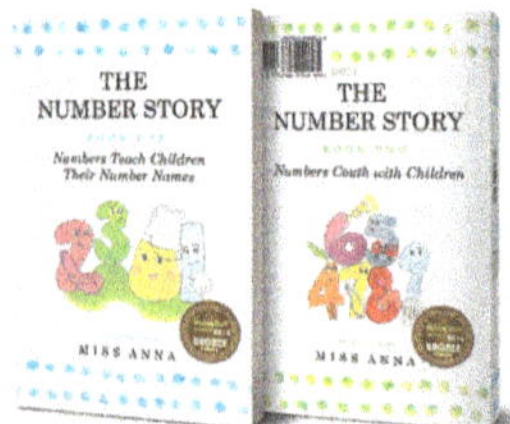

Number Story 1 & 2
isbn: 978-0-996216-48-7

Numbers 11-20
& Ordinals
first, second, third...

Number Story 3 & 4
isbn: 978-1-945977-01-5

Numbers 0-100
& Place Values
ones, tens, hundreds...

Number Story 5 & 6
isbn: 978-1-945977-06-0

About Clocks
& Telling Time
hours, minutes, seconds...

Number Story 7 & 8
isbn: 978-1-949320-40-4

For more Miss Anna books to love,
visit us at

www.missannabooks.com

Numbers are working hard all over the world!
Come Travel the World with Us!